# Animal Attack and Defense

# AMAZING ARMOR

Kimberley Jane Pryor

**Marshall Cavendish**
Benchmark

New York

This edition first published in 2010 in the United States of America by
MARSHALL CAVENDISH BENCHMARK.

MARSHALL CAVENDISH BENCHMARK
99 White Plains Road
Tarrytown, NY 10591
www.marshallcavendish.us

All Internet sites were available and accurate when sent to press.

First published in 2008 by
MACMILLAN EDUCATION AUSTRALIA PTY LTD
15–19 Claremont Street, South Yarra 3141

Visit our website at www.macmillan.com.au or go directly to www.macmillanlibrary.com.au

Associated companies and representatives throughout the world.

Copyright © Kimberley Jane Pryor 2009

Library of Congress Cataloging-in-Publication Data

Pryor, Kimberley Jane.
    Amazing armor / by Kimberley Jane Pryor.
        p. cm. – (Animal attack and defense)
    Includes index.
    Summary: "Discusses how animals use armor to protect themselves from predators or to catch prey"–Provided
by publisher.
    ISBN 978-0-7614-4424-4
    1. Body covering (Anatomy)–Juvenile literature. 2. Animal defenses–Juvenile literature. 3. Animal weapons–
Juvenile literature. I. Title.
    QL941.P79 2009
591.47'7–dc22
                                                                                2009004996

Edited by Julia Carlomagno
Text and cover design by Ben Galpin
Page layout by Domenic Lauricella
Photo research by Claire Armstrong and Legend Images

Printed in the United States

**Acknowledgments**
The author and the publisher are grateful to the following for permission to reproduce copyright material:

Cover and title page photo of a short-beaked echidna © Steven David Miller/Auscape

Photos courtesy of: © Peter Fakler/Alamy/Photolibrary, **30** (right); © Kevin Deacon/Auscape, **25**; © Steven David
Miller/Auscape, **30** (left); © Johannes Gerhardus Swanepoel/Dreamstime.com, **6**; © Zepherwind/Dreamstime.com,
**5**; © Getty Images/Dr Dennis Kunkel, **20**; © Getty Images/Panoramic Images, **14**; © Getty Images/Photolibrary,
**9**; © Getty Images/Jeff Rotman, **29**; © Getty Images/Hans Strand, **8**; © Getty Images/Tom Walker, **7**; © Gina
Hanf/iStockphoto.com, **13**; © Constance McGuire/iStockphoto.com, **26**; © James Riley/iStockphoto.com, **19**; ©
Jon Maloney, www.jdmpics.com, **10**; Photolibrary/Lind a Freshwaters Arndt, **28**; Photolibrary/Andrew Bee, **21**;
Photolibrary/Perrine Doug, **11**; Photolibrary/David B Fleetham, **23**; Photolibrary/Paul Freed, **22**; Photolibrary/
Martin Harvey, **16**; Photolibrary/Luiz C Marigo, **17**; Photolibrary/Tom McHugh, **24**; Photolibrary/Photo Researchers,
**18**; Photolibrary/Ron Sanford, **15**; Photolibrary/Kurt Scholz, **27**; Photolibrary/Konrad Wothe, **12**; © Ferenc Cegledi/
Shutterstock, **4**.

While every care has been taken to trace and acknowledge copyright, the publisher tenders their apologies for any
accidental infringement where copyright has proved untraceable. Where the attempt has been unsuccessful, the
publisher welcomes information that would redress the situation.

For Nick, Ashley, and Thomas

1 3 5 6 4 2

# Contents

## Glossary Word

When a word is printed in **bold**, you can look up its meaning in the glossary on page 31.

# Types of Armor

There are many different types of armor in the animal world. Some types of armor are used for stopping predators in their tracks. For example, predators might be **wary** of approaching an animal with armor such as vicious spines or a thick shell. Some types of armor are also used to fend off attacks. For example, sharp teeth can cut through a predator's skin, and razor-sharp claws can rip flesh from bones.

The longhorn cowfish's body is protected inside an armored box.

# How Armor Protects Animals

Armor helps animals to protect their bodies and defend themselves against **predators**. Animals with armor do not have to move as quickly or be as alert as other animals. They can move around their **habitats** freely because their armor protects them from many predators.

A seahorse has bony rings of body armor to stop predators from eating it.

## Vital Statistics

- **Height at shoulder:** up to 4.9 feet (1.5 meters)
- **Habitat:** forests and plains
- **Distribution:** Africa
- **Predators:** lions

## A Cape Buffalo's Horns

A cape buffalo's heavy horns curve down, then up and in. In males, the two horns are joined by a boss, which is a shield that covers the head.

# Cape Buffaloes

Cape buffaloes are massive animals with heavy, **ridged** horns. If they are hurt, they become one of the most dangerous types of animals in Africa.

Cape buffaloes are fast, powerful, and aggressive. When they are wounded by a predator, cape buffaloes charge furiously, with their horns held high. At the last moment cape buffaloes lower their horns and toss their victims into the air.

A cape buffalo can charge at enemies with its heavy, ridged horns held high.

6

Male moose fight each other in the breeding season for the right to mate with female moose.

# Moose

Male moose have antlers that are up to 5.9 feet (1.8 meters) wide. They have very few predators because of this powerful armor.

Male moose often battle fiercely for female moose in the breeding season. They bring their antlers together and push each other with them until one moose backs down. The winner gets to mate with the female. The loser is sometimes badly injured or even killed.

## Vital Statistics

- **Height at shoulder:** 4.9 to 6.6 ft (1.5 to 2 m)
- **Habitat:** forests
- **Distribution:** Europe, Asia, and North America
- **Predators:** tigers, wolves, and bears

## A Moose's Antlers

Only male moose have antlers. A moose's antlers are grown in spring and **shed** after the mating season each year. They grow to full size in just a few months.

## A Walrus's Tusks

Both male and female walruses have tusks. A male walrus's tusks grow to 3.3 ft (1 m) in length and weigh 11.9 pounds (5.4 kilograms) each.

# Walruses

Walruses are armed with long, hard tusks. Male walruses sometimes use their tusks to stab **rival** males.

The largest male walruses have the longest tusks, and they are the most aggressive. They display their tusks to scare smaller males into giving up their resting spots. In the breeding season, male walruses compete for the right to mate with female walruses. They stab each other in the neck with their tusks.

Male walruses attack rival males with their long, hard tusks.

A warthog's sharp, pointed lower tusks are more dangerous than its curved upper tusks.

## Vital Statistics

- **Height at shoulder:** 2.5 ft (76 centimeters)
- **Habitat:** grasslands
- **Distribution:** Africa
- **Predators:** crocodiles, hyenas, lions, and leopards

# Warthogs

Warthogs use their tusks as deadly weapons. They can inflict deep wounds with their sharp lower tusks.

Warthogs run away or back into their burrows when in danger. If warthogs are cornered, they attack predators with their tusks, while squealing at the tops of their lungs. Males sometimes fight other males for the right to mate with females in the breeding season.

## A Warthog's Tusks

Both male and female warthogs have tusks. The tusks in a warthog's lower jaw are extremely sharp. The curved tusks in a warthog's upper jaw may grow to 2 ft (60 cm) in length.

# Gaboon Vipers

## Vital Statistics

- **Length:** 6.6 ft (2 m)
- **Habitat:** tropical forests
- **Distribution:** Africa
- **Predators:** none known

## A Gaboon Viper's Fangs

A Gaboon viper has the longest fangs of any **venomous** snake. Its fangs can grow up to 2 inches (5 cm) in length.

Gaboon vipers are deadly snakes. They use their long fangs to inject **venom** into their victims. Gaboon vipers produce more venom than any other snake.

Gaboon vipers lurk in leaves on the forest floor and **ambush** their **prey**. When Gaboon vipers strike, they open their mouths to let their fangs swing forward. Then they sink their fangs into their prey and venom flows down the fangs.

A Gaboon viper's huge fangs can inject enough venom to kill a human adult.

## Vital Statistics

- **Length:** 19.7 ft (6 m)
- **Habitat:** cool waters
- **Distribution:** cool coastal waters worldwide
- **Predators:** other sharks and whales

A great white shark has huge jaws with rows of razor-sharp teeth.

# Great White Sharks

Great white sharks are the most feared sharks in the ocean, due to their powerful jaws and teeth. They are also known as "maneaters" and "white death."

Great white sharks roam the world's oceans in search of food. They charge at victims from below. As great white sharks bite their prey, they shake their heads violently from side to side. This causes their **serrated teeth** to saw chunks of flesh from the victim.

## A Great White Shark's Teeth

A great white shark has extra rows of teeth to replace teeth that get pulled out or damaged. It has up to 3,000 teeth at any one time.

11

An Australian magpie's powerful beak is so sharp that it can pierce human skin and draw blood.

## Vital Statistics

- **Length:** 1.2 to 1.4 ft (38 to 44 cm)
- **Habitat:** woodlands
- **Distribution:** Australia
- **Predators:** lizards and owls

## An Australian Magpie's Beak

An Australian magpie's strong, straight beak is designed for probing into soft ground and grasping prey. It is also used for fighting, and can injure and even kill another bird.

# Australian Magpies

Some male Australian magpies fiercely defend their nest and the area around it during the breeding season. They swoop on, and peck at, any animal that threatens their territory, nest, mate, or chicks.

Australian magpies are aggressive only during the breeding season. Some Australian magpies attack people traveling past their nest. Australian magpies swoop on their victims, beating their wings loudly and clacking their beaks. They sometimes give their victims a hard peck on the head.

# Macaws

**M**acaws have very powerful beaks. They can crush things with incredible force.

Macaws are colorful and clever birds that are sometimes kept as pets. They sometimes attack people who do cruel things, such as pull their long tails. Because their beaks are so big and powerful, macaws can cause serious injury to children and adults.

## Vital Statistics

- **Length:** 1 to 3.3 ft (30 cm to 1 m)
- **Habitat:** forests
- **Distribution:** Central and South America
- **Predators:** snakes and birds of prey

## A Macaw's Beak

A macaw's strong, curved beak is designed to crush nuts and seeds. It can even crush very tough nuts, such as brazil nuts.

Macaws can crack open very tough nuts with their powerful beaks.

A grizzly bear defends itself with its huge paws and powerful claws.

## Vital Statistics

- **Height when standing:** 8.2 ft (2.5 m)
- **Habitat:** forests, mountain slopes, and river valleys
- **Distribution:** North America
- **Predators:** none known

## A Grizzly Bear's Claws

A grizzly bear's powerful claws are up to 5.9 in (15 cm) in length. They leave deep gashes when a grizzly bear scratches trees.

# Grizzly Bears

Grizzly bears are enormous animals that most people would not want to meet in the wild. Females with cubs are the most dangerous grizzly bears.

When grizzly bears are taken by surprise, they either flee or stand their ground. Grizzly bears will attack to defend their cubs or their food if they feel threatened. They charge at predators at speeds of up to 30 miles per hour (48 kilometers), and attack them with long claws and sharp teeth.

# Peregrine Falcons

Peregrine falcons are awesome hunters with huge talons. They can kill other birds with one fierce blow from their **clenched** talons.

Peregrine falcons defend their nests and territory against foxes and other large birds of prey. They dive on animals much larger than themselves. They grab animals with their powerful talons and slash them with their strong, hooked beaks.

## Vital Statistics

- **Length:** 1.6 ft (48 cm)
- **Habitat:** rocky open country near water
- **Distribution:** all continents except Antarctica
- **Predators:** foxes and other birds of prey

## A Peregrine Falcon's Talons

A peregrine falcon's curved talons are deadly weapons. They can kill another bird almost instantly.

A peregrine falcon can swoop on predators and attack them with its talons.

# Kangaroos

Male kangaroos kick with their back feet when they fight rival males.

Kangaroos look soft and cuddly. However, they kick with their powerful back legs if they feel threatened.

Kangaroos lean back on their thick, strong tails and kick forward with their back legs. Their kicks are so powerful that they can knock humans to the ground. A kangaroo's sharp claws can rip open an animal's flesh.

## Vital Statistics

- **Height when standing:** up to 6.6 ft (2 m)
- **Habitat:** woodlands, grasslands, and deserts
- **Distribution:** Australia
- **Predators:** wild dogs called dingoes and other dogs

## A Kangaroo's Feet

A kangaroo has long, narrow back feet and its fourth toe is long and powerful. A kangaroo's toes have very sharp claws.

# Giraffes

Majestic giraffes defend themselves with their strong hooves. A giraffe can shatter an animal's skull or break its spine with one hard kick.

Few predators dare to take on giraffes, because they are difficult and dangerous prey. Giraffes are tall, and they kick with great force, especially when defending their calves.

## A Giraffe's Hooves

A giraffe's hooves are known as cloven hooves because they are split into two parts.

A female giraffe kicks with her back feet to defend herself.

17

# Aardvarks

Aardvarks are solid, medium-sized mammals. Their main protection is their super-tough skin.

Aardvarks are **nocturnal**. They awaken in the evening and set out to find food. They tear ant and termite nests apart with their powerful claws. When the insects stream out, aardvarks lap them up with their long, sticky tongues. Their thick skin protects them from painful insect bites and stings.

## Vital Statistics

- **Length with tail:** 5.9 ft (1.8 m)
- **Habitat:** forests and plains
- **Distribution:** Africa
- **Predators:** snakes, lions, leopards, and hunting dogs

## An Aardvark's Skin

An aardvark's pale yellow-gray skin is very thick. The skin has a thin covering of coarse hairs.

An aardvark's tough skin protects it from insect bites when it burrows in insect nests.

A rhinoceros is protected by its tough skin, which has lots of wrinkles and creases.

# Rhinoceroses

Rhinoceroses are massive animals that sometimes charge without warning. They are protected by very thick skin.

Rhinoceroses have poor eyesight, but excellent senses of hearing and smell. If a mother with a calf senses a predator, she lowers her head, snorts, and charges. She **gores** the predator with her long horns. Her thick skin protects her from large teeth and sharp claws of predators.

## Vital Statistics

- **Length:** 8.2 to 14.1 ft (2.5 to 4.3 m)
- **Habitat:** forests, grasslands, and swamps
- **Distribution:** Africa and Asia
- **Predators:** lions

## A Rhinoceros's Skin

The thick, protective skin of a rhinoceros forms large folds, especially at the shoulders and thighs. The skin is hairless, except on the tip of the tail and in the fringes of the ear.

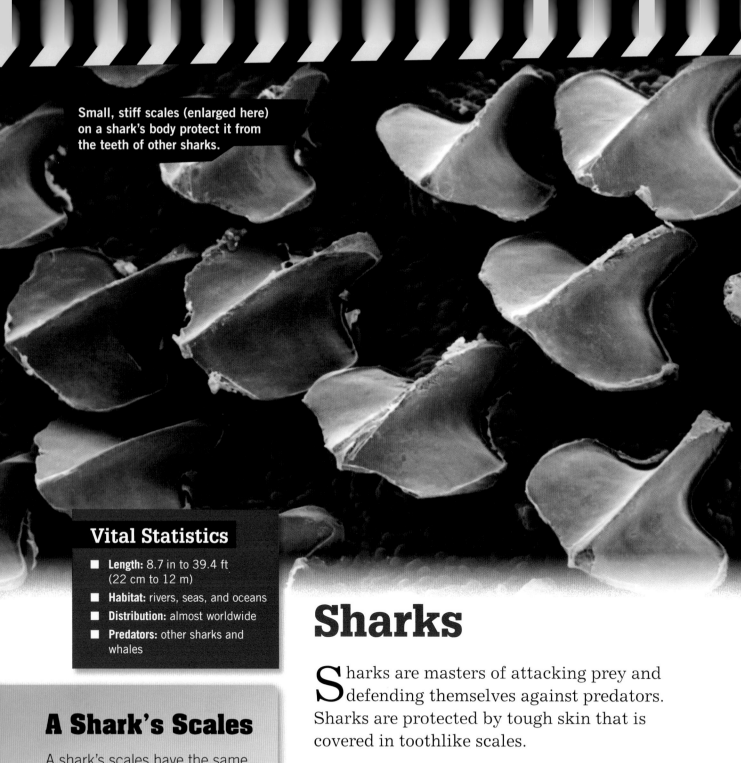

Small, stiff scales (enlarged here) on a shark's body protect it from the teeth of other sharks.

## Vital Statistics

- **Length:** 8.7 in to 39.4 ft (22 cm to 12 m)
- **Habitat:** rivers, seas, and oceans
- **Distribution:** almost worldwide
- **Predators:** other sharks and whales

## A Shark's Scales

A shark's scales have the same layers as human teeth. Each scale has an inner core of pulp, a middle layer of dentine, and an outer layer of enamel.

# Sharks

Sharks are masters of attacking prey and defending themselves against predators. Sharks are protected by tough skin that is covered in toothlike scales.

A shark's toothlike scales allow it to move through the water easily. Scales also allow it to swim quietly toward unsuspecting prey. Scales protect a shark from the wild chomping of other sharks during a feeding frenzy.

# Snakes

Snakes are clever hunters that track, catch, and eat living animals. Their scales protect them from predators, from injury, and from drying out.

Many snakes have spectacular patterns, which are formed by different skin colors showing through their clear scales. Patterns allow snakes to blend in with their surroundings so they are not seen by predators or prey.

## Vital Statistics

- **Length:** 3.9 in to 23 ft (10 cm to 7 m)
- **Habitat:** forests, woodlands, grasslands, deserts, swamps, rivers, and oceans
- **Distribution:** almost worldwide
- **Predators:** other snakes, birds, badgers, weasels, and mongooses

## A Snake's Scales

A snake has two main kinds of scales. Smooth scales are shiny. Keeled scales are rough and have a ridge down the center.

Snakes regularly shed their outer layer of scales in one piece.

# Southern Three-Banded Armadilloes

## Vital Statistics

- **Length with tail:** up to 1.1 ft (35 cm)
- **Habitat:** grasslands and marshlands
- **Distribution:** South America
- **Predators:** jaguars

Southern three-banded armadilloes have two special ways to protect themselves from predators. Not only do they have armor covering most of their bodies, they can also roll themselves up.

All armadilloes have armor made of plates that are covered in scales. However, a southern three-banded armadillo can also roll itself into a tight ball. This hides its soft body parts from predators. The southern three-banded armadillo's head, legs, and tail all fit inside the armored plates.

## A Southern Three-Banded Armadillo's Armored Plates

A southern three-banded armadillo's armor is on the head, back, and tail. The armor is made of solid plates separated by movable bands.

The armored plates on the head, back, and tail of a southern three-banded armadillo fit neatly together to form a ball.

Armored plates protect a chiton's soft body.

**Vital Statistics**

- **Length:** up to 1.4 ft (43 cm)
- **Habitat:** rocky shores
- **Distribution:** worldwide
- **Predators:** sea stars, octopuses, fish, and seabirds

# Chitons

Chitons are oval-shaped sea animals. Their armored plates give them very good protection from predators.

A chiton has many defenses against predators. Its armored plates hide and protect its soft body. Its large, flat foot grips rocks with surprising strength. A chiton can also roll up its body.

## A Chiton's Armored Plates

A chiton has a shell made from eight overlapping plates. They are held together by a tough structure known as a girdle.

# Crabs

Crabs scuttle over sand and rocks with their large claws ready to defend themselves from predators. Their bodies are protected by broad, flat, hard coverings.

A crab sheds its hard covering when it needs to grow. It has a new, bigger covering underneath. At first the new covering is soft, and the crab is **vulnerable** to predators. However, the new covering quickly hardens.

## Vital Statistics

- **Width:** 0.4 in to 13.1 ft (1 cm to 4 m)
- **Habitat:** mangroves, coasts, and oceans
- **Distribution:** warmer parts of the world
- **Predators:** octopuses, fish, birds, monkeys, and seals

## A Crab's Hard Covering

A crab's hard covering is called a carapace. It protects the crab's head, **thorax**, and **gills**.

The Japanese spider crab's hard carapace measures 1.2 ft (37 centimeters) across.

# Lobsters

Lobsters have very thick, hard coverings. Their hard coverings are made up of many smaller sections.

True lobsters have enormous claws on their front pair of legs. These claws can give predators painful nips. Spiny lobsters and slipper lobsters do not have claws. Their only defense is their hard coverings, which protect them from predators.

## Vital Statistics

- **Length:** 0.7 to 3.3 ft (20 cm to 1 m)
- **Habitat:** ocean floor
- **Distribution:** all oceans except polar oceans
- **Predators:** octopuses, fish, and turtles

## A Lobster's Hard Covering

A lobster's hard covering protects its head and thorax. It also protects its gills, which are attached to the bases of its legs and the sides of its body.

A spiny lobster's hard covering protects its soft body from predators.

## Vital Statistics

- **Length:** 4 in to 6.6 ft (10 cm to 2 m)
- **Habitat:** ponds, lakes, and oceans
- **Distribution:** warmer parts of the world
- **Predators:** fish, sharks, crocodiles, snakes, raccoons, and whales

## A Turtle's Shell

A turtle's shell is made from two parts: the carapace, which covers the top of the turtle, and the plastron, which protects the bottom. The parts are connected at the sides.

# Turtles

Turtles have lived on Earth for more than 200 million years. They have a strong protective shell that provides them with a good defense against predators.

A turtle's shell is made from sixty bones covered with horny plates. The shell is attached to a turtle's spine and ribs, so that it cannot crawl out of it. Some turtles pull their heads straight back into their shells in order to hide from predators. Some turtles fold their necks sideways instead.

# Giant Clams

Colorful giant clams are the largest and heaviest **mollusks** in the world. They have thick, heavy shells to protect their soft bodies from predators.

A giant clam opens its shell during the day and spreads out a soft part of its body, called the mantle. If disturbed, the giant clam pulls the mantle back in and closes the shell to protect itself from predators.

## Vital Statistics

- **Length:** 3.9 ft (1.2 m)
- **Habitat:** coral reefs
- **Distribution:** Indian and Pacific oceans
- **Predators:** fish and rays

## A Giant Clam's Shell

A giant clam is known as a bivalve because its shell has two equal parts. The parts are joined by a hinge made of muscle.

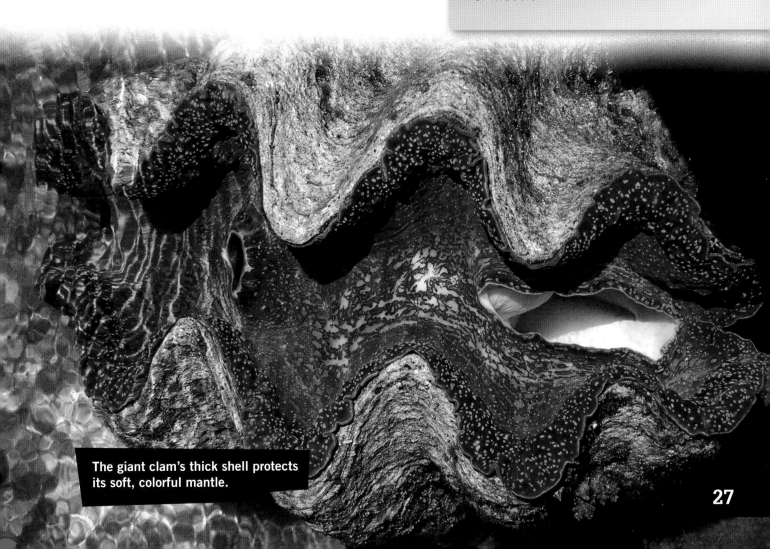

The giant clam's thick shell protects its soft, colorful mantle.

27

A North American porcupine with raised quills looks much bigger than another with its quills lying flat.

## Vital Statistics

- **Length with tail:** 3.1 ft (95 cm)
- **Habitat:** woodlands
- **Distribution:** North America and Central America
- **Predators:** birds of prey, fishers, coyotes, wolves, mountain lions, and bobcats

## A North American Porcupine's Quills

A North American porcupine's quills are stiff hairs with tiny barbs on the ends. They are about 3 in (75 millimeters) long.

# North American Porcupines

North American porcupines have about 30,000 large, sharp spines called quills. These spines cover their upper bodies, from their heads down to their tails.

When a predator approaches a North American porcupine, the porcupine turns away. Then it raises its quills and slams its powerful tail into the predator. Some of the quills come away from the North American porcupine's body and stick into the predator's flesh. The predator has no way of removing them, and may eventually die.

# Sea Urchins

Sea urchins are covered with long, strong spines. Most predators stay away from them.

Sea urchins are not aggressive animals. The danger comes when someone touches or steps on one. A sea urchin's sharp spines puncture the skin and sometimes break off in the wound. They often cause severe pain and infection.

## Vital Statistics

- **Spine length:** up to 1 ft (30 cm)
- **Habitat:** rocky ocean floor
- **Distribution:** worldwide
- **Predators:** fish, wolf eels, and sea otters

## A Sea Urchin's Spines

A sea urchin's spines are long and thin, like needles, or short and thick, like pencils. Sea urchins use their spines to move around, as well as to defend themselves.

Sea urchins use their sharp spines for protection against predators.

# Double Defenses

Many animals have not just one, but two ways
to defend themselves from predators.

# Short-Beaked Echidnas

Short-beaked echidnas have excellent
defenses. They use armor and tricky
behavior to defend themselves
against predators.

## A Short-Beaked Echidna's Armor

A short-beaked echidna has long, pointy
spines all over its back and sides. If
disturbed, it curls into a prickly ball to
protect its soft belly.

## A Short-Beaked Echidna's Tricky Behavior

A short-beaked echidna can dig straight
down into the soil until only its spines are
showing. It can also wedge itself tightly into
rock crevices and hollow logs by stretching
out its legs and spines.

| | |
|---|---|
| **ambush** | attack after lying in wait in a hiding place |
| **clenched** | partly closed |
| **gills** | parts of the body that some animals use for breathing under water |
| **gores** | pierces or stabs |
| **habitats** | areas where animals live, feed, and breed |
| **hooves** | tough coverings that protect the toes or feet of some animals |
| **invertebrates** | animals without a backbone |
| **mollusks** | animals with soft bodies, that may or may not have a shell |
| **nocturnal** | active during the night |
| **predators** | animals that hunt and kill other animals for food |
| **prey** | animals that are hunted and caught for food by other animals |
| **ridged** | having narrow, raised strips |
| **rival** | an animal that wants the same thing as another animal |
| **serrated teeth** | teeth with notches or sharp edges |
| **shed** | fall off when no longer needed |
| **talons** | the sharp claws of a bird of prey |
| **territory** | an area occupied by an animal, a mating pair of animals, or a group of animals |
| **thorax** | the middle section of the body of some invertebrates |
| **venom** | a type of poison |
| **venomous** | being able to make a type of poison called venom |
| **vulnerable** | likely to be hurt |
| **wary** | careful or cautious |